TOWARDS HOME

Joy Graham Riggs

Copyright © 2023 Joy Graham Riggs.

All rights reserved. No part of this book may be used or reproduced by any means, graphic, electronic, or mechanical, including photocopying, recording, taping or by any information storage retrieval system without the written permission of the author except in the case of brief quotations embodied in critical articles and reviews.

LifeRich Publishing is a registered trademark of The Reader's Digest Association, Inc.

LifeRich Publishing books may be ordered through booksellers or by contacting:

LifeRich Publishing
1663 Liberty Drive
Bloomington, IN 47403
www.liferichpublishing.com
844-686-9607

Because of the dynamic nature of the Internet, any web addresses or links contained in this book may have changed since publication and may no longer be valid. The views expressed in this work are solely those of the author and do not necessarily reflect the views of the publisher, and the publisher hereby disclaims any responsibility for them.

Any people depicted in stock imagery provided by Getty Images are models, and such images are being used for illustrative purposes only.
Certain stock imagery © Getty Images.

ISBN: 978-1-4897-4741-9 (sc)
ISBN: 978-1-4897-4740-2 (hc)
ISBN: 978-1-4897-4836-2 (e)

Library of Congress Control Number: 2023911945

Print information available on the last page.

LifeRich Publishing rev. date: 06/28/2023

Contents

I. The Beginning 1
II. Growing Up 11
III. The Day of Adversity 19
IV. It's All About Me 33
V. Falling From Grace 41
VI. A Place of Healing 59
VII. Earthquakes 67
VIII. Haight-Ashbury or Finding Our Place in the World 79
IX. Finishing the Race 91
X. What I Think I Have Learned 97
Bibliography 107

I
The Beginning

Each of us is defined by the time and place we occupy at any given moment in our lives. No matter how insignificant we may believe ourselves to be, we are part of a ripple of cause and effect that determines events and shapes our lives and the lives of others. There are unseen forces that buffet us to and fro. How we choose to respond to these forces are the choices we must make. Some of us search for wisdom and direction from a creator that must exist. Others run without rhyme or reason, letting the flow take them where it will.

The assassination of Austrian Archduke Franz Ferdinand on June 18, 1914 was considered to be the catalyst for World War I. On June 24, 1917, American troops arrived in France to join the battle. On that same day in Corsicana, Texas my mother was born.

It was one hundred degrees and my grandmother had told her six-year-old daughter, Clearcy, that there was a golden ring behind the picture on the wall. If Clearcy would just fan her a little bit longer, my grandmother would get it for her when she could get out of bed.

My grandmother was dying from what was called "child bed" or puerperal fever. Most births took place at home at that time. Sterilization was an issue, along with all the other myriad things that can go wrong as life is passed from one generation to the next. Antibiotics were not invented until 1930 and infections caused high fevers, which frequently led to death within hours or days of giving birth. She would linger in that heat from inside and outside of her body for eighteen days before she died.

I remember visiting my mother's family one hot summer day when I was a little girl. We walked through the cemetery where my grandmother was buried and searched for her grave for what seemed like an eternity. I felt an unfamiliar sadness that was as oppressive as the heat and buzzing insects. The fact that she had died did not sadden me as much as the time it took for us to locate her grave. How could they have forgotten where she was laid? Her tombstone indicated that she was twenty-seven. "Faithful to her trust even unto death" was inscribed above the dates February 28, 1890–July 13, 1917.

Attempting to keep her memory alive, I tried to picture in my mind what it must have been like for her. I remember the pale pink roses on the faded green paper that covered the walls in the room where she died. Thin white wires were stapled above the wide white baseboards. The wires bringing electricity would have been added long after the house was built and my grandmother could have benefited from the cooling relief that modern invention would have brought.

There were long, low windows and the beadboard covered ceilings always seemed so high to me. The exterior of the little house was painted a bright, clean white and it had a nice wide porch across the front. My grandfather was often sitting there in his rocker when we came up to visit him. He had outlived two wives by then and was alone.

He was always smiling and he had what my father called the "gift of gab." His white shirts and dark pants were always clean and pressed. I think it is easier to stay clean in that part of Texas where the dirt just blows off. We lived near Houston, where the frequent humidity seems to make dirt stick. Sometimes he wore a hat—not a cowboy hat, but a hat like the men wore in the movies in the fifties. It occurs to me that we usually visited on a Sunday, so he probably hadn't changed his clothes since he came home from church.

I had heard the story about the ring behind the picture many times when we visited my mother's birth family. However, my aunts never said which picture was thought to harbor that ring. Was it the picture of Jesus standing at the door symbolizing the human heart and knocking? That dime store picture was as common in Protestant homes as pictures of the Virgin Mary were in Catholic homes back then. I had seen it many times when we visited.

Maybe it was the old sepia-toned photograph of the young family as it was before my mother's birth and her mother's death. It would have been of my grandfather, General Wheeler (why anyone would name a baby boy General is beyond me), my grandmother Gayley, and their four little girls: Velma, Clearcy, Vesper, and Ruby, aged seven, five, three, and one, respectively.

Photographs can never reveal the true story of the people that they capture in that moment of time. We can only imagine what their lives and their true personalities were like. I have a photograph of my grandparents as a young couple. It may have been their wedding photo. I'm not sure. My grandfather was fairly handsome. At least, I thought so. He had thick, sandy colored hair that was parted on the side. His jaw was somewhat square and he looked straight into the camera. His eyes appeared to be brown and his suit was tan.

I thought my grandmother was lovely with dark hair pulled back from a forehead that was smooth and proud. Her face was almost a perfect oval. She did not look into the camera. Her eyes were downcast and she seemed to be looking off into the distance. You could still tell that her eyes were large, light colored, and a little sad. She wore a white blouse and a black skirt fitted to her trim waist. Neither of them was smiling, but I don't think they smiled for photos back then because they had to sit so still. They would both have been in their early twenties.

I see echoes of their faces in the faces of my sisters and me, my children, grandchildren, nieces, and nephews. We are all as different as snowflakes, but do the stories of our ancestors form an almost collective memory that flows from generation to generation? Are our attitudes just modeled on what we see lived out before us? Where does faith become our own? Is there more to empathy than just empathy? If God says he will judge the nations, does that suggest a shared mindset? If nations are invaded, will the mix change them substantially? If our heritage is lost, who or what becomes our guiding light?

I am sure a thorough search was made for that ring by the older girls. If Clearcy couldn't find it, Velma could. I believe they would have called Aunt Velma a precocious child. My grandmother had said she wouldn't mind dying if she could take Velma with her. It may have been delirium talking, but since she died before she could explain her reasoning, the family was left to wonder. Had she said this because she would miss her oldest daughter so much? It is more likely that, because she was such a headstrong child, her mother doubted that anyone else in the family could handle her.

God says He fashions us in the womb, so he must fashion our personalities as well as our physical attributes. Maybe those traits of children that reduce their parents to tears are the very ones that will see them through the storms that lie ahead for them. The trick is to teach children to be civilized without destroying the gift inside.

It was decided that in order to spare Velma further shocks, she would not be allowed to attend her mother's burial. Resenting the fact that she would have to stay home with her younger sisters, she took matters into her own hands. The cemetery was not too far from their house, so Velma walked, unseen, to the fence enclosing the area. She climbed a nearby tree and from that lofty vantage point, she watched the process play out.

Those little fingers, holding onto that rough bark, with

jaw set in determination and tears streaming down her cheeks was how I pictured her. What did she think or feel up there on that limb without an adult to comfort her or explain things? Maybe she felt closer to heaven and her mother from that height where she was "above it all."

My son-in-law maintains that children are rubber and they tend to bounce so they are less likely to get hurt from tumbles and falls. Emotional events are the true shapers of our lives and write on our souls in a language only God can understand. Having been a less than perfect child myself, I can imagine that Velma may have made some pretty tall promises to God out there, suspended between earth and sky. As an adult, she became an Assembly of God preacher and traveled the preaching circuits with her husband, Hoke Hunter.

I remember my four aunts as adults. Aunt Velma had fair skin, wavy brown hair, blue eyes, and straight, white teeth. She reminded me of June Carter Cash, who sang country and western songs with her husband, Johnny Cash, in the late fifties and early sixties. Aunt Vesper looked a lot like her, just a little softer. Both of them were taller than their sisters. Aunt Clearcy and Aunt Ruth were smaller and dark eyed. My cousin Joe, Aunt Ruth's son, said they looked like two sets of twins. They did not and I told him he was silly.

They didn't live near our family. We lived in a small

town close to Houston and my mother's sisters still lived in and around Corsicana. I assume that is why we got the doll and my cousin Joe and his sister Ruby got the pony.

For Christmas one year, Aunt Vesper sent us a large "Baby Coo" doll. She did not have children of her own and she always sent us the best gifts. I was about four when we got him and I remember that he was almost as big as me. My sisters were eight and eleven. He had a blue crocheted cap and overalls. Only someone who has grown up in a family of just girls can understand the novelty of getting a boy doll instead of a curly-headed girl doll in a frilly dress again.

It was not that we didn't appreciate our other dolls, but Timmy was special. Aunt Vesper, being from a family of girls herself, understood this. We loved her for it—and no, dolls were not anatomically correct back then.

Our cousins, however, got the pony. It seems that she, Aunt Vesper, had given them a pony and it was too young to ride. It was too far to walk home with it, and since they didn't have a trailer, she devised a plan. They somehow maneuvered that pony into the backseat of her Cadillac with its front legs draped over the front seat and its rump on the back seat. She drove it to their house.

Our adult cousins told us this story at a family funeral many years later and I have no cause to doubt them. The last time I heard of Aunt Vesper, her husband had died and she had remarried and was moving to Alaska. Once, she came to visit our mother. Mother did not get many visits from her birth family. The times we visited them were often memorable and not in a good way.

I think that Aunt Clearcy, the daughter who was promised the ring, became the caretaker of the family. She took care of their dad until he went into a nursing home, where he married for the third time. She also cared for Aunt Vesper when she became frail. There was not much mention of caregiver burnout back then.

Aunt Ruby was the youngest until my mother was born. She was pretty and adventurous, taking up smoking at a young age. She married a man who was several years older than she was and they had a boy and a girl. I thought my heart would break for him when she died at the age of forty-two. Through tears, he said, "I never dreamed she would go before me."

They owned or managed a hotel in the city and after the funeral, he brought the families there to eat from a large steam table. I don't think they were one of the "Twenty-one," but they were probably close.

According to the Texas State Historical Association, by the 1890s, oil was taking over from agriculture in Corsicana. Because of the influx of people, they needed to expand the existing water supply. They dug for water and hit oil and gas. They had five wells in 1896 and fifty-seven the following year. By 1898, there were 287 producing wells.

The second oil boom came in 1923 with the Powell oil field, and they had to put up street lights to control the traffic. During the oil boom, the population stood at about 28,000, but dwindled when the wells slowed down and the depression hit. There was a rebound during the war, and by the early fifties, they estimated there were no less than twenty-one millionaires in town. The median income in 1953 was $1,222.00 and claimed to be the highest in Texas. In 1956, they hit a new oilfield in East Corsicana and within a month, there were 500 producing wells, nearly one in every backyard.

II
Growing Up

With their mother gone, the girls stayed with their Aunt Alice and her husband Bud for a while. Their father G.W. had remarried to a very good woman named Eunice. She must have been a gift from God for that family because the girls grew to adulthood without great mishap. When it was time for them to return home, Aunt Alice said, "I can't give the baby (my mother) back. I'm the only mother she has ever known and I love her like my own." She had weaned her son, Walter, from her breast to nurse her. My mother became the fourth child in that family of her cousins. The line-up was Clara Mae, Grady, Walter, and my mother Oleta. Uncle Derwood and Aunt Frankie Jeane (Bobby) would be born later.

Our Uncle Walter and his wife Doris had five girls who were roughly the same ages as my sisters and me. When we got together, we were a gaggle of eight little girls, all within eight years of each other. Ida Jo, Janie, Betty, Emma

Joyce, and Judy were our partners in crime and secrets were guarded like in the Mafia. Once, when we hadn't seen them for over a year, Betty made sure to tell us that our secret hiding place was still "a secret." A boy, Walter, was added to their family much later and, somehow, he made it to adulthood in that ocean of estrogen.

My sisters and I have so many memories of these cousins. They are all tied up with family holidays, summer visits, and shared secrets. A few years ago, we saw three of them at a family reunion and suddenly, we were all children again, despite our haggard bodies and grief-worn souls. Two special memories are a balm for darker days, even now. The events were mundane, but an unexpected joy permeated our beings.

Our families went out to Old River, a recreational area, one summer night. It had a large concrete pavilion that served as a dance floor. We were the only people there and our parents turned on a car radio. Pairing off, we started to dance to the old honky-tonk tunes as we sang. "Your cheatin' heart will tell on you" bounced off the ears of the listening pines. Gingham checked dresses, hand-me-down blue jeans, and bare feet twirled in and out of the moonlight under the shadow of the trees. The water on the nearby lake glistened, and even the mosquitos, which could be as big as horseflies, gave us a beak that evening.

The second memory is just as earthshakingly simple. We

had gone to visit them at their farm in Madisonville and went to see a new calf in the pasture. It was probably less than a half mile from their house, but for short little legs, it seemed like Dallas. It started to rain so hard that the raindrops stung as they hit your face. Ida Joe, the oldest, told us to run for the hay house. We all wrestled the big, wide doors shut on their track near the ceiling and we were safe from the deluge.

The walls were made of dark, thick, pine logs. Sweet smelling bales of hay were stacked at various heights around the floor. We each found a comfortable niche and settled in for the siege. We stayed there for hours, waiting for the rain to stop, singing songs and telling ghost stories. When the older girls started to talk about boys, my younger cousins and I drifted off to sleep.

A few years ago, my youngest grandson went to church camp. He was asked to pray and said, "Dear Lord, thank you for letting us be here at camp without our parents." That made me think about our hay house adventure. No parents were there to tell us what to do or say. Time was inconsequential. It was a brief paradise in a world mostly filled with care and confusion.

Why do childhood memories hold such wonder? In Matthew 18 (KJV), Jesus says that if we expect to enter heaven, we must be like little children. He says that their (children's) angels behold the face of the father all day.

Who are these angels and what is so special about a child? I know that it is easier for a child to trust and to be comforted than an adult. Children are not so quick to judge, and they accept even the warts on a frog as fascinating and wonderful. Will that unbridled joy that only children can feel be a prerequisite for entrance into paradise? Will He replace the wonder that we have lost like a badge given at the door of a convention?

He says in that same chapter that if anyone harms those "little ones" who believe in Him, it would be better for that person to have a millstone hung about his or her neck and be tossed into the sea. In John 15 (KJV), He calls His disciples "my little children." We have to give up a lot of pride and notions of our own wisdom to follow like children; this becomes increasingly harder as we get older. Only when our lives become "train wrecks" do we revert back to the helplessness of children and admit our inadequacies. I believe every human disaster can prove to be a stepping-stone to God. It's all about where we put our eyes, as they used to sing on *Sesame Street*.

Returning to my mother's saga, her adopted family of cousins was not as well off as her birth family. The three boys were a little wilder and woollier than her sisters. As Shakespeare would say, "there's the rub."

My mother lived with her cousins but spent some summers and holidays with her sisters. My grandfather was a devoted family man and deacon for his church. Although perfection doesn't have a home on this planet, he and Eunice raised the girls to be responsible and modest in their dress.

At this time, however, skirts were getting shorter and short (bobbed) hair was the latest thing. I think Aunt Bobby was the first to get that short hairdo, and that was where she got her nickname. The cousins were making the jump into the "roaring" thirties, but the sisters were not there yet, at least not openly.

My mother told us about going to visit her father and sisters when she was about thirteen. She was wearing a short skirt and was immediately given a longer, more modest one to change into. When it was time for her to go home, the short skirt was nowhere to be found.

There was a constant loosening and tightening of the reins as far as my mother was concerned, and it must have set up some instability in her. Most likely, there was some resentment on the part of the other children from both families. Her sisters may have seen her as a little of an intruder with special status, and the cousins may have resented the times she was able to get new things they couldn't afford. Uncle Bud became ill and couldn't work. The depression began to tighten its grip, and there was less and less to go around, especially for the cousins. When my mother told us her biscuit story, we were indignant at the injustice of it all.

It seems that she was hungry, and while she sat at her desk, she pinched off a piece of biscuit that she had brought for lunch. Her teacher saw her and said, "Oleta, you can come up here in front of the class and eat that biscuit." She did so with tears running down her face, and she was so humiliated she didn't want to go back to school.

The cousins picked cotton, and Aunt Alice, it was said, could barter with the best of the men for a good price. Later, she became a practical nurse, and much later she dabbled in real estate near Houston. She was a strong woman, and my mother loved her. When Clara Mae went to college to get a teaching certificate, my mother, who was fourteen at the time, went with her. They were allowed to stay in the dorm and work at "light housekeeping" to pay their way.

It was a good time of life for my mother. She graduated as salutatorian of her grade school and played basketball. She was tall with long, skinny legs. My father teased her and called her "Skeeter" because of those legs, which earned him a gesture that he long remembered.

My dad's family was fairly "well to do." Mother said she prayed it wouldn't rain when he came over to see her because they had a tin roof. I don't think he cared.

My father's family consisted of him, his brother Leo, my grandfather Barney, and grandmother Aunt Thelma. Uncle Leo was the oldest and he was about six feet five, weighing about 300 pounds. My dad was only five eleven and weighed a little over 200 pounds, so his brother called him "sister" Altie. His name was Altus. Uncle Leo was larger than life in so many ways. I don't think I ever saw him when he wasn't smiling and joking. This was in sharp contrast to my grandfather, who seldom smiled. My biological grandmother had died when my father was fifteen and his brother was seventeen. I have only seen pictures of her and her family. They were tall, substantially built people, and I believe they were of Dutch descent.

A few years after my paternal grandmother's death, my grandfather married a young neighbor woman. Because she was twenty years his junior, his sons declined to call her mother. Uncle Leo's three boys and my sisters and I were taught to refer to her as Aunt Thelma and she wore that moniker graciously. Aunt Thelma was small, dark, and plain with very bad teeth, but she was also beautiful. When our family came to visit, she lit up like a Christmas tree.

She was a good cook and I remember a knife she used to cut up sausage. The blade was so worn that it formed a crescent. Their home was old and large, but very clean. It had a wide porch on three sides with thick columns and gingerbread trim. It needed paint, but was otherwise spotless with a manicured lawn.

There was a door on one side that was always kept locked. It had a white porcelain knob and strange smells emitted from the threshold. I had imagined all sorts of creatures and other things too horrible to contemplate lurked within the dark recesses of that room. I later learned it was storage for potatoes, onions, and other vegetables from their garden. We lived in the city.

Early on, they had an outhouse and I remember the smells from that place too. When they did add an indoor toilet, I think they added it to what had been the dining room. It was so intimidating to try to use the facilities in such a wide-open space. A large table and old-fashioned icebox with punched tin on the front was the only other furniture in that room.

One night, I slept on a cot in the front room as my Grandpa Graham and Aunt Thelma sat talking and drinking coffee at another large table. My eyes were shut, but I wasn't yet asleep. She said, "Just look at her, Barney. Ain't she a pretty little girl." I heard him mutter, "Yeah."

I was skinny with mousey brown hair and wore blue glasses because of a lazy eye. They were often smudged and were always slipping down my nose. My mother accused me of hiding my eyes behind those glasses more than once. Aunt Thelma, however, thought I was pretty and she was also a star in my heaven.

III
The Day of Adversity

Proverbs 17:17 of the King James Bible says that a brother is born for the day of adversity. I am sure this applies to sisters too. The adverse becomes less traumatic when you have someone to share it with. Sometimes we laugh, then cry together at what cannot be changed and must be accepted. My oldest sister, Trisha, would tell her friends that we were too poor to have a brother. We were not poor; we would probably have been considered middle class. My father had told us that you need a sense of humor to get through life and I think that became her mantra. When a friend asked if she had naturally curly hair, she replied, "You don't think I would do this to it on purpose, do you?"

    I have two sisters and they were indeed born for the day of adversity. Only when you grow old do you appreciate the richness and all things wonderful that siblings bring into your life. They can get you into trouble at the drop of a hat, but they can also help "fade the heat" when things get rough. This is one of my favorite pictures of my mother and sisters. I was born a few months after it was taken.

Trisha's given name is Patricia Jeane. Her friends called her Pat, and the family called her Trisha. She is seven years older than me. The smartest and the most gregarious of us, she was a joiner in school and probably belonged to a dozen clubs.

Trisha was a really cute little girl with green eyes, curly, light brown hair, dimples, and a smile that turned up a little on one side. She had a mischievous twinkle in her eye, and she was as obstinate as Aunt Velma. My mother related the time that three-year-old Trisha left the yard when mother was hanging out clothes. A man who knew the family recognized her and brought her back home from the steps of a nearby college. She was therefore the first of us to approach academia.

On another occasion, a relative commented on what a sweet little girl she was and touched her dimple. She bit him. She made good grades and liked to flaunt her extensive vocabulary. She would say, "Joy Lynn, you are a non-compass menace, and you belong in an eleemosynary institution." In reply I would begin to swing my seven-year-old arms at her like a windmill, and she would hold me by my head so that I couldn't reach her body.

When she grew up, her blond hair became brown, and she was a little busty, which she did not appreciate. She was about five feet six inches tall, and a little overweight in a Marilyn Monroe sort of way. If I had told her that, she might have smacked me. I thought she looked nice in her sweater and scarf, paired with the circle skirts that were the style in the mid-fifties. She even had one with a poodle on it.

As she became a teenager and Mother experienced her first in a series of hospitalizations, my dad depended on her more and more. He would ask her, "How was your mother today?" whenever he got home from work. He bought her a car: a red, second-hand Chevy, which she and her friends named Suicide because the passenger door had a tendency to fly open when a right-hand turn was made. She got into trouble because they liked to play "Chinese fire drill." They would stop at a red light and everyone in the car, usually four or more, would get out, run around the car, and get back in before the light turned green.

Since it was a second-hand car, Suicide had some flaws. There was rust on the inside metal part of the door panels that extended about four inches below the windows. It was summer, and Trisha had bought some red paint. In an unusually inclusive mood, she even let Cindy, our other sister, and I paint some of this metal trim.

I think it was probably more a Tom Sawyer moment, but we would have given her an apple to paint, for sure. After the painting was done, which we thought looked pretty good for a brush job, we went inside to watch *Sky King* on the TV until mother sent us to Miller's Grocery for something she needed.

Suicide had a tendency to stall. As a standard shift, it could be pushed while someone popped the clutch, and the car would start. She stalled, as usual. Cindy and I got out to push, and as she jerked into motion, the doors, which also had a tendency to stick, swung shut. We each put one hand on the handle and the other onto the door through the open windows for balance. The car lurched again and we held on to keep our footing, pulled on the doors again, and hopped inside. When I think about the incident, I can almost feel the red paint sliding under my fingers, forever ruffled and fingerprinted, a testament to plans gone wrong and Murphy's law.

There were so many memories tied to that car. When Mother had her first few hospitalizations, she would come home free from her delusions and very tranquil—too tranquil. The Thorazine gave us all some peace, but made her a little zombie-like. Later, as I became an occupational therapist, I learned it was called the Thorazine shuffle.

Trisha and her friends Joyce and Reba would pick up Mother after school and take her with them to get a Coke. I know she enjoyed those little excursions back into society and it helped rebuild some of the mother/daughter relationship between Trisha and her, although it would forever be reversed.

It was especially hard on Trisha when Mother began to manifest her illness, probably because she, being about thirteen when it started in earnest, was old enough to understand how much Mother was changing.

Cynthia and I were about ten and six, so her illness was our reality for a few years, and we believed most of her delusions were gospel. Trisha had to make the difficult choice of whether she would confront Mother when she told her to do something or argue with her. Sometimes she argued when Mother was right and Trisha was wrong.

Like all teenagers, she wanted a little more freedom than she could handle at times and probably thought she deserved it for all the responsibility she had shouldered. Her favorite reaction was to run upstairs to her room and hit the light switch so hard that she broke it more than once. My dad was an electrician and had wired our house with a new kind of on/off switch that had a flat plate and not a toggle. It didn't hurt her hand, but the switch would be smashed.

Teenagers don't always get the credit they deserve. Since emotional instability is their bedrock, they are uniquely positioned to understand emotional turmoil. Compassion for others is more accessible in their natures than for most adults who have long since turned off some of those feelings.

When she was about eighteen, Trisha met a guy through one of her friends who was dating his younger brother. His name was Don and he was about five years older than she was. Don was thin and had black hair that was always neatly combed and held in place with a lot of hair oil. He had done a brief stint in the Navy and had broken his nose, which did not make him less attractive, only more interesting. He usually wore short-sleeved button-up shirts and blue jeans, but occasionally he wore a clean white t-shirt with a pack of cigarettes rolled up into the sleeve. His pointed toe cowboy boots were always polished.

I was eleven when they started dating and he would tease me mercilessly. Therefore, when he would knock on the front door, I would open it and hit him in the stomach. I never really hit him hard, but he would double over like I had hurt him.

I thought he was too skinny, so it became my routine to fry thin sliced potatoes for him whenever he came over. His mother said she did not know if he came to see me or Trisha. It must have been her because they were married a year later.

Don was always kind and understanding with our mother, and she loved him. She was never above pointing out what she considered an indiscretion in any of us, but he always took it graciously.

My other sister is Cynthia Anne, who we called Cindy. She dethroned Trisha as the only child and "better her than me." Cindy was the most precious little girl. She was very blond with blue eyes and the sweetest smile. You would have thought she would break if you touched her too hard. She was always very quiet and shy—such an angelic, delicate little girl.

Trisha hated her. Mother would have to spank her to let Cindy walk to school with her, but all of that turned around when they were in high school. They became close friends and would sometimes put on their gym shorts and do exercises in Trisha's room. Of course, they were talking shop and discussing boys.

In the summer especially, the bedroom door would stick, and it served to keep me out. I would tell on them and Mother would make them open the door. After a few minutes of suddenly dull conversation, I would get bored and leave the room.

It seemed like Cindy was always the one to be hurt. She acquired two small scars on either side of her forehead, but you wouldn't know they were there unless you really looked for them. She accidently hit me in the nose with a softball once, but other than that nothing noteworthy happened to me.

The acquisition of her first scar occurred on a rainy day as we were leaving the house for school. We were late, and Mother was telling us to hurry up and get in the car. Once again, we had an issue with a sticking door. The kitchen door had a large pane of glass, and this was before safety glass. Trisha slammed the door. The glass came down, and Cindy had to get stitches. Yes, it could have been so much worse, but drama is drama.

The second injury occurred during a Stanley home party that our mother was hosting. The women were inside looking at stuff, and the kids were running around in the yard outside. Someone got the bright idea of filling glass

Coke bottles with water, shaking them up, and throwing the water on each other. One of the boys came around a corner. Cindy came around from the other side and was conked in the head. As the women led her into the bathroom and she bled over the toilet, one of the ladies related how she had gotten a fishing hook caught in her back and how they had to dig it out. The more she talked, the more Cindy threw up.

When we were younger, Cindy became my surrogate mother. I would tag along with her wherever she went. I went with her to her friends' houses, to the neighborhood pool, and to the movies. When she and Zelda walked across the street during evening church services to get a Coke at the drugstore, I was there. I never told. She had another friend who would always take my glasses off and clean them whenever she saw me.

Cindy taught me so much, like the fact that we all have a twin somewhere in the world who looks just like us. They usually live on the opposite side of the world, so we don't see them. Ours would probably be in China. The eye difference was not an issue.

For many years, I thought Cindy was a little "dingy" for this revelation until I saw a PBS (Public Broadcasting System) documentary about quantum theory. As my limited brain power understands this theory, for every action in the world, there is a proposed mirrored action somewhere else in the world, but it only comes into being when it is recognized or detected by us. We only see the second in response to the first. Maybe that *would* suggest that we have twins somewhere. I imagine one of her teachers may have used this illustration to explain the theory on a rudimentary level.

This theory was in contrast to Einstein's theory of relativity that says each action has an equal but opposite reaction, not a mirrored one. Using that logic, it appears to me that if a pimple arises somewhere in the universe, a dimple must come into being somewhere else. Quantum theory seems to me to suggests a magic mirror trick: it's only there when it's twin is there. If the light goes out in one part of pair, it's dark somewhere else in response.

I do not claim to understand these theories, but they are said to be the underpinnings of computers. My husband took computer classes in college and explained to me that the messaging between computers has to do with some combination of zero and one, and on and off patterns. I would think that smoke signals had a similar pattern of communication, so how advanced are we really.

The PBS documentary went on to suggest that in trying to understand the makeup of the universe, physicists attempt to understand the mind of God and His creation. I am aware that it is the nature of humans to create and discover. Proverbs 25:2 (KJV) reads, "It is the glory of God to hide a thing, but the honor of kings is to search out a matter." I think this is no longer the goal.

Many seem to want to recreate what God has done. I think their choice of building materials, wires, chips, and other components seems crude. It reminds me of the joke about the man who says, "I can create anything God has created." He reaches down to pick up some clay to begin his building and a voice says, "Not so fast. Get your own dirt."

Our building materials lack the "good stuff" and will never result in a valuable product. It isn't really about the conduit or method of delivery on the information highway where we find ourselves that is the problem. The stuff that flows through it or on it is toxic. Our world wide web is a horizontal Tower of Babel. It is an attempt to tear down and rebuild creation and assert human beings as the supreme beings. We (humankind) seem to say that we can remake ourselves and our universe. We can control it all. It sounds so familiar. We already fell for this once, and making the apple shiny and fast won't help us digest the coming consequences.

The preceding paragraphs represent going off on a tangent. Now I will tangent back to my story.

Cindy also became my moral compass. I once broke a bracelet when we were taking a nap. We always napped on the floor because Mother did not want to remake the beds. In the days before extensive use of air conditioners, when attic fans were the antidote to the Texas heat, it was cooler on the floor also. I hid the broken bracelet under the bed and then said I had lost it. Cindy told on me in order to save my soul and it taught me a lesson. I don't hide things that I have broken under my bed to this day.

She was never mean to me, and in some rare cases, it paid off for her, I think. She had a crush on a boy who worked at the concession stand at the local movie theater. Standing behind the popcorn machine, she would watch him, but did not dare speak to him. One evening, just before closing, as we waited for our ride home, I struck up a conversation with him. It quickly escalated to a war of insults like, "You are so ugly, I bet you have to sneak up on a glass of water to get a drink" and "You are so ugly, you look like you've been hit with an ugly stick." These were from a comedian who was popular at the time, and we continued until we ran out of material.

Cindy came out from hiding and laughed with us. Our ride was late and we were almost the last to leave. He asked for her phone number, and I quickly gave it to him. There were a few more crushes before the great and notable days of Max.

Kids used to go outside and play in their yards. Imagine that. We had a stump in our backyard. We would play king on the mountain and push each other off. We would also pretend to be Sheena, queen of the jungle. We would command our slaves to bring us various things. I knew something was up when, for the third time, Cindy said, "Bring me Max."

Max was the cousin of Trisha's friend Reba, and they had classes together at school. He had come to our house to get an assignment from Trisha, and Cindy opened the door. She was barefooted, wearing her white gym shorts and one of our dad's old shirts which she and Trisha often commandeered. He was smitten at first glance.

She and Max started dating when she was fourteen, and he was seventeen. He, like Don, was skinny with black hair and blue eyes. He was very tall, six feet three inches, and could sing like Elvis. He and Don each had a black fifty-seven Chevrolet. We had a two-story house, and when my dad thought it was time for the guys to go home, he would bang on the floor upstairs. Max was known to squeal his tires when he left.

When they married three years later, it was payback time for me. I was in charge of my nephew Brad when they came home to visit. He always wore cowboy boots, and his legs were never still. I even had to take him with me on a date because they said it was my turn because I had gone with them on so many of theirs.

IV
It's All About Me

When I was in college, one of our activities was to try to connect with our earliest memories. Mine was from when I was about two years old. It was late fall or winter because it was cold outside. We were returning from a trip in our car, and it was early evening. I was being carried into the house half asleep and was placed on my parents' bed. They had a dark purple silk comforter, and it was drawn up over my body and tucked in at the sides. As I drifted back to sleep in that cool, dark room, I felt the smooth silk against my skin as my body warmed to the cocoon created for me. I felt loved and protected against the world. No harm could come to me. Peace filled my universe.

Since I was the youngest child and a little prone to getting my own way, I was to experience a hard stop in my willfulness when I was about six. My sister Cindy and our neighbor, another girl named Joy, were sitting on the front porch talking. I wanted to be with them, but they told me to go away and play with Joy's little brothers, who were about three and five.

I came up with a brilliant plan. I would spank the little kid and make him cry, then I would tell the girls that he had hurt himself. They would hold him and baby him like they always did and I would get to be the hero. This would buy me some time in their honored presence.

I took him into the open garage, put him over my knee, and gave him a couple of whacks. He started to cry, and the game was on until doomsday arrived. My mother rounded the corner just in time to witness the aggression. Before I could say, "But Mom, the girls wouldn't," I was in our house. I got a spanking with one of my father's leather belts that hung from the closet door. Then, I was made to take a bath and put on clean clothes even though it was the middle of the day.

My father did not attend church with us. He was raised a Methodist, and my mother was a Baptist, but twice on Sunday and most Wednesday nights would find the rest of us there.

On one particular Sunday evening, about a year after the incident, as I sat next to my mother, our preacher delivered a sermon with my name all over it. He talked about sin and how we are all guilty before God. If God doled out our just punishments, none of us would survive. Jesus took our punishments on him because he could take it. He loved us so much and missed us so much that He had made a way for us to come to Him.

Jesus had done His work and was not here now, but He had left us a comforter, His Holy Spirit. Now I knew about the evil that lurked in me personally, and I also knew what a comforter was. I remembered that cold day and the purple silk against my skin.

I was wearing a gray plaid skirt with red threads running through it. My knees were shaking so badly that the plaid seemed to dance. I told my mother that I wanted to "go up front." My friend Janice was sitting beside me, and Mother suggested that she go with me so I wouldn't be scared. It didn't matter to me if Janice went or not, but she did. I was young and only understood the very basics, but that belief in a loving God was about to see me through some stormy days ahead.

It probably helped that I had an earthly father who loved me too. I don't think men always realize how much their presence means to their families. Just being there speaks volumes without a word being uttered.

The picture that follows is not of very good quality, but if you are able to read the body language, you can recognize the protection and safety that my sisters and I felt from our father. He has a hand touching each of us. He used to tell us, jokingly, that he was glad all his boys were girls. When his grandsons made their appearance, I felt he may have been overcompensating a tad. He seemed awfully proud all his boys were boys too. This is a picture of my family about five years before my mother's illness began to take shape. Our mother looks a little distant to me. There seems to be a slight separation in the family unit, nothing that you would ever pick up on unless you had an eye into the future. Maybe I'm looking for something that is not really there, but I don't see a totally cohesive group.

When I was about nine, I was invited to go home after school with Kay. She was not really my friend, and I was a little surprised when her mother picked us up after school. After we got to their home, we looked at her dolls for a little while, and then Kay showed me their special room.

It was pretty, but a little vanilla. There was a very clean beige carpet that looked like it had seldom been walked on, a beige sofa and chair that looked like they had seldom been sat on, and a Bible on the coffee table that looked like it had rarely been opened. We were not supposed to be in that room, and she knew it.

In that quiet, solitary place, Kay said, "My mother says you're crazy like your mother." Granted, I probably was an odd child with nervous ticks, but my only thought was that it took her what seemed like an eternity to draw a capital K. We were learning to write cursive and I could finish a sentence, dot every i and cross every t before she laid her pencil down. I'm not saying that she was slow, but she was not the sharpest tool in the box and she was rude. My mother was not crazy either.

I felt like she was calling me stupid. I think people do equate mental illness with inferior intelligence, but when it is not combined with developmental delays, this is not true. Sometimes, even people with delayed cognitive development seem to have a clearer picture of what it takes to get along in the world. They show a greater natural or unschooled intelligence than those who succeed on a material or educational level.

Reviewing, in my own mind, whether I might not be up to par in the brain department, I began to consider my assets. I made As and Bs in school. I knew that I was good at drawing, and my mother had told me that it was a special gift to be able to see beauty where other people may not see it. I won a fire prevention poster contest that year for the fourth through sixth grades. I drew a campfire with crossed logs in the center. The flames were blue, yellow, orange, and red. There was a slogan in each corner like, "Only you can prevent forest fires" and "Drown all campfires." I won five dollars and bought a pair of roller skates with the money.

Paper dolls were also my specialty, and the other girls in the class lined up for me to make ones for them. I drew the dolls in underwear using a heavy stroke of the pencil. Then I placed another piece of paper over that one and, tracing the shape of the doll underneath, I would draw dresses and other outfits. Tabs on the shoulders and waist held the clothes onto the dolls after they were cut out. I don't know how we got away with it, but I only remember getting into trouble once.

The point is that only we can evaluate our worth, not other people. There is value in our uniqueness. We can learn from others, refining the final product a little, but changing to please someone else or for the sake of change is counterproductive and self-destructive.

In hindsight, I realize that I was probably sent home with Kay because my mother was being admitted to the hospital again. My father and Kay's father were both electricians in our small town, and they knew each other well. My father would need to stash me somewhere out of the way temporarily.

When my mother's pattern of hospitalizations became established, I tried to make sense of the "why" of it. If God was in control and worked for the good of his children, then what was His purpose in this? I rationalized, in my child's mind, that there may have been people at the hospital she needed to share her faith with, but I missed her and needed her.

One case in point is when I was in the sixth grade and joined the band. We marched on the field for the first time. We were not in junior high yet, so there were no uniforms for us. We needed white shirts and blue jeans. I had a white shirt, but no blue jeans. I borrowed a pair from my older sister, but since they were too big, I turned them inside out and stitched them by hand from the waist to the hem. As we marched, the stitching came undone, but luckily the waist was still intact when we returned to the bleachers. Later, I took homemaking in high school and became a proficient seamstress, always remembering to check for loose threads.

V

Falling From Grace

How can I describe my mother without prejudice? I obviously can't. Half our being comes from each parent biologically or by example in the case of adoption. It takes a lot of abuse over a lot of years for a child to become bitter about a parent. Even then, we generally stand ready to forgive and treasure the valuables that remain of that life-forming relationship.

I thought my mother was very pretty. She was five feet five inches tall and had long, thin legs as mentioned before with the "Skeeter" comment from my father. She had dark brown hair and green eyes. Her face shape was a perfect oval, like the pictures of her mother, and her forehead was smooth and clear. Most of the time, she wore her hair pulled back behind her ears and held in place with bobby pins.

Soft curls escaped from her temples and fell onto her brow. Her lips were slightly full and she had a sweet smile that at the same time suggested a little mystery. Her lips turned down slightly at the corners, and there was just a suggestion of dimples.

I remember her wearing heels and a slim, dark skirt with a cream-colored swing coat that ended just below the hips. She was graceful and stood with her shoulders straight, but not stiff. On her lapel was a turquoise brooch made in the shape of a daisy. She had gone to John Robert Powers Modeling Studio, and she and my sister Cindy had been asked to audition for pictures to appear in a Foley's Department Store ad, but she didn't follow through with it. She also took bookkeeping classes for a few months.

For several holiday seasons, she worked at Kresses' department store behind the candy counter. My dad took us there one December, just before Christmas, and bought us a little red plastic sleigh with eight white reindeer tied on with white ribbon. Santa sat on the seat and there was candy in his bag in the back. It is such a vivid memory.

When life was sweet and uncomplicated, my dad would come home from work and kiss my mother on the cheek. I would drop my eyes and say, "You don't love me anymore." Then, of course, he would kiss me too. Their arguments were pretty tame back then. Sometimes she would drive her point home with, "Now listen here, big boy" like Elizabeth Taylor in the movie *Giant*. All in all, I think the love they shared seemed superhuman. It kept our family together when those around were falling apart. God doesn't take us out of the storms; He walks beside us through them.

Mother had a tattered spiral notebook of poems that she had written. Here are two of my favorites.

Little Man
No worries, no cares my little man
As you dream of the future to be.
The cities bright lights that hold so much
And the ships sailing out to sea.
May you always have such faith and hope
In a world of toil and strife.
For this is the makings of a wonderful man
In this thing we call life.

The Farm
To be awakened in the morning by the
old cock's continuous alarm
All the chores must be done before sunup
That's a life on the farm
But when the grass is newly mown
And the fields are a verdant green
It holds more beauty to me
Than all the city lights I've seen

I suppose the real change in my mother started after her hysterectomy, when she was thirty-seven. I was about six and my sisters were ten and thirteen. They performed a total hysterectomy, which means they removed her uterus and her ovaries as well.

Currently they try to spare those organs because it causes a loss of hormones and catapults the woman into instant menopause, which normally can take many years to navigate. Two of her friends also had this surgery at about the same time. Each of them had brief mental breakdowns also as a result, but nothing like my mother's.

I have since learned in my college classes about the delicate balance between physical, mental, and social factors in our lives. Although pain and excessive bleeding may be stopped, menopause affects the inner workings of the mind subtly. The woman loses some of her sense of well-being, body routines are changed, and there is a knowledge that an important defining period of life has ended. Self-doubt can creep in, coloring how we feel about our value to other people, and in the extreme, our right to exist at all.

Condense all these factors into a period of a few weeks and it can be devastating. Depression and anxiety can remain long after. Hormone therapy has come a long way, but as with all of life's challenges, the spiritual component may be overlooked or denied altogether.

I believe this operation was not the cause, but a contributing factor to my mother's illness. Whatever the trigger, changes were coming for our family, and none of us would ever be the same.

My mother had been all about saving money. She starched and ironed my father's khaki work clothes instead of sending them to the cleaners and we ate a lot of beans and cornbread for supper. Bologna sandwiches were our staple for lunch. A mustard and sugar fold-over sandwich was our favorite snack as kids.

On paydays, however, she would splurge and buy Cokes and Fritos. They used to sell six-ounce bottles of Coke in a twelve pack, and there was a small celebration when we came home from school on Fridays.

My dad had bought a small air conditioner and put it in the dining room window so he could have some relief from the heat when he came home from his electrical business for lunch. Mother would wait until the last minute to turn it on because she thought it would make our electrical bill too high. It took a little while for the room to cool off, and there was an ongoing battle over the timing of that switch.

One of the first changes we saw involved finances. She went to Foley's department store and charged several hundred dollars' worth of glassware. That was a lot of money in the late fifties. My dad made about seventy dollars a week, and we were considered middle class.

There were bowls, sets of drinking glasses and a really pretty ashtray with swirls of color blown into the glass. One of us still has the green cake stand with the clear pedestal. It must be Cindy.

We never were quite sure who my mother would be on any given day. Sometimes she was so agitated you couldn't rest around her. Sometimes she would sit in her chair, perfectly still, for hours; this is called catatonia. She may have been hearing voices.

Becoming extremely jealous, she accused my father of so much infidelity he would need a stunt double. Thinking she could read the thoughts of other people she would frequently tell us to clean up our minds as we sat watching TV. More often, this was directed at my sisters since they were old enough to know the "facts of life." She accused them of being streetwalkers, which I thought was funny since they were almost always home, especially after dark. If she herself had what she considered to be an evil thought, she would say, "Out the window, bless."

She developed a persistent delusion about the Catholic Church that was situated across the street from a vacant lot behind our house. I later learned from my psychology classes that all delusions are founded in reality, which the mind rewrites.

The reality soil that grew my mother's delusions had to do with the difference between Catholic and Protestant theology. Both the Catholic and Protestant faiths are rooted in Judaism. The Protestants broke away from the Catholics in the 1500s when Martin Luther nailed his ninety-nine theses to the door and condemned the sale of indulgences. This was the practice of buying another person's soul out of purgatory by contributing to the church. He interpreted the scriptures as saying that we are saved by grace through the blood of Christ and not by works, so there was no need for deeds or money given to the church to be absolved from sin.

The Protestant faith also holds that Christ is the only intercessor between God and man. There is, therefore, no need for a priest or pope to grant forgiveness or absolution. We are taught to call no man "father," for the scriptures state that there is one father, and he is God. To bow before or to kiss the ring of the pope is to put him before Christ.

The book of Revelations, the last book of the Bible, states that in the last days an anti-Christ will come onto the world stage and declare himself to be God. A false prophet will be at his side. Some thought the pope could be such a prophet. Later, a psychiatrist would ask our mother, "Mrs. Graham, don't you think the Catholics have as much right to live as you?"

My mother began to think evil messages were being sent through the air from that church behind our house. She feared that they would come through the window of the bedroom where my sister and I slept. She would have us pull our mattresses off the beds onto the floor. Sometimes, we would wake up in the middle of the night, and she would be sitting at the foot of our bed, watching out that window. This, of course, meant that she was not getting any sleep. Later, she would identify this as a factor leading to her illness.

I don't remember the exact studies, but I know that lack of sleep for an extended period of time leads to psychosis. I pray for all those new mothers who choose to or out of necessity need to hold down a full-time job.

Maybe it was because we believed our mother's delusion or maybe there was some other cause for the noises, but my sister and I could, at times, hear quiet whispering noises at night, and they did not come from our mother. I used to irritate Cindy by mimicking the whispers, and she would threaten me if I didn't stop.

Young children tend to adopt their parents' beliefs. I remember that I used to make faces at one of my teachers in school because my mother had made some disparaging remarks about her. I did get over it, however, once I felt safe in that classroom and actually liked her. She must have had some inside information about my situation.

Early intervention is an important part of therapy for children, but I think they would have locked me up and thrown away the key if they had tried to intervene in my thought processes at that time. Experience and maturity need time to do their part where young children are concerned.

From my own experiences as a therapist, I know how quickly we like to wrap things up and write our notes, but life is messy and things just take time. Some kind of family therapy is always more appropriate with children, if possible. It prevents driving a wedge between the child and a family they will probably still have to live in.

The one incident that may have put the cork in the bottle for my mother had to do with a neighbor. This woman liked to go around the neighborhood and visit, gossiping as she went. My mother didn't gossip, and sent this woman on her way.

We had a big Pontiac car. My uncle Leo had a car dealership in San Antonio, and always gave us a good deal on the price. One day, this neighbor was leaving another neighbor's house. We had just left our driveway, and she was almost in her yard. She looked back at my mother and gave her a smile that was more of a smirk. Mother gunned the motor, and the woman jumped the curb into her yard. Her eyes were as big as saucers.

Shortly after that, two men pulled up in our yard in an ambulance and came into our house without knocking. They each put a hand on our mother's arms and began to take her down the stairs. Cindy and I started to kick and hit them with all the fury a seven-year-old and eleven-year-old could muster. A short while later, our father came home. He must have tried to explain things to us, but all I remember is the hatred I felt for him at that time.

Our Aunt Bobby came to spend a few weeks with us while Mother was hospitalized. Later, she said she did not see how any of us had any sense at all. I could not sit still and talked incessantly. She wanted to spank me, but my sisters wouldn't let her.

Aunt Bobby believed that our mother was always a little different, and she also felt that she never recovered from the death of her older sister and mother's cousin, Clara Mae. She was the cousin mother had stayed with when she went to college.

Clara Mae was pregnant and expecting her first child when she went into premature labor. She was given an injection to stop the contractions. This sent her into convulsions, and she chewed her tongue before she died. Near the end of her life sixty years later, my mother would call out for Clara Mae as she slept and dreamed.

Our mother came home after about two weeks and was calmer, even if she seemed a little over-sedated. She seemed almost "normal," and things would rock on until the agitation and delusions would start to return. Her hospitalizations were always brief, probably because of finances, and resulted in several return visits over a period of about seven years.

She had shock treatments, which would cause short-term

memory loss. Ironically, she later said that they did help a little. Maybe they interrupted her thought patterns and gave her a brief respite from her torments, but eventually the madness would creep back in. When she was truly ill, her eyes would become glassy. She had some insight and called it a wild look. I remember that I loved to go to school where there was some predictability.

During the times that she was hospitalized, my sisters and I grew closer to our dad. He took us shopping for school clothes one year. We went to Robert Halls in Houston, which was a step up from Weiner's and the other places Mother had shopped to save money

My mother had always dressed me in dark clothes, because she said they looked better against my dark complexion, but that year it was all about the pastels. One outfit consisted of a solid blue blouse with puff sleeves and a Peter Pan collar coupled with a blue print skirt that had a thin belt with a little silver anchor dangling off the buckle. The other outfit was a pink checkered skirt and a white Angel blouse. It was gathered a few inches below the neck and had wide lace trim at the elbow length sleeves and the bottom. I felt so special in those outfits. The best part was that my dad was part of the process.

Mother had been diagnosed with schizophrenia. I could never list all the studies that have been conducted over the years to identify a cause for this condition. Suspected causes have included poor infant nutrition during the first three months of life, genetics, abuse, poverty, environmental pollution, demonic possession, brain injury, physical injury, isolation, and so much more.

Since the current treatments were not working as well as hoped for her, a newer in vogue method was suggested. Pre-frontal lobotomies had been used to help uncontrollable patients become more manageable and her doctors thought it would be worth a try. For this procedure, they essentially take a long probe, insert it into the frontal lobe of the brain and twist it, severing the nerves that connect that part of the brain to the rest.

Some had said it was like taking a sledgehammer to the brain and yet others said it saved their family members from suicide or helped them become more emotionally stable. It did not, however, change delusional thinking. The reasoning here was similar to shock treatments. It was supposed to interrupt the pathway between the seat of emotion, the prefrontal lobe, and the planning, reasoning part of the brain. Unlike shock treatments, it was permanent.

It generally left the person with blunted affect (flat expression) and the inability to become emotionally stressed. It also took away some of the higher thinking skills such as planning, and some people became more impulsive and lost sexual inhibition. They became childlike and docile, but dull.

For my mother, it did release her from some of her emotional turmoil, so something was improved. It seemed that she still became agitated, but the anger and desperation were not there. Her facial expressions were blunted and she was a little impulsive. She liked to move the furniture around, a trait which I have inherited. On one occasion, I helped her move a large credenza from the dining room to a room upstairs. I bet it weighed 300 pounds. What the mind can conceive, the body will try to do.

The delusions were probably still there, but they weren't worth the emotional energy to follow through on them. When I worked at the Harris County Psychiatric Facility as an adult, one of the doctors advised a long-time patient, "Just don't tell people you hear voices." This patient was no danger to himself or others, and light conversation was possible, but if you scratched the surface, you would find all kinds of interesting things.

I think this was one of the most sensible strategies I had heard in that setting. Sometimes other people have to change, and we have to let loose of our preconceived notions of what is normal. If Mohammad won't come to the mountain, the mountain may have to move a little.

By the time I was in high school, a few friends from the band would come home with me on football Fridays, and we would leave for the band hall from my house. We lived across the street from the stadium and about a block from the school. They talked about how sweet my mother was, and what a good listener she was, unlike their parents. During my senior year, my best friend moved in with us because her parents were getting a divorce, and she wanted to get away from all the stress. That was how far we had come by that time.

However, going back about four years, there was still a little more dancing with the devil to do. He seemed to love to come and visit our family when he was bored.

Shortly after my mother's surgery, my father landed a big contract to wire the new football stadium that was being built across the street from where we lived. Once it was finished, people would ask if they could park in our driveway on football nights. Sometimes they just blocked off the exit with their cars and we couldn't get out.

For this job, new aluminum light poles were used. My dad said the older wooden poles held the iron foot pegs screwed into them better. They went deep into the wood, whereas the foot pegs for the aluminum poles were held in place with aluminum screws.

He was about thirty feet up in the air wiring one of these poles. He unbuckled his safety harness so he could pass under a bar that held the pole to the stadium bleachers. The aluminum foot peg broke off the pole, and he fell.

I was leaving our house to walk to his shop to bring lunch to my sister Cindy, who was answering phones for him. I watched as this khaki-colored bag fell onto the concrete below. My brother-in-law, who was working for my dad, was trying to jump a barbed-wire fence to get to our house to call an ambulance. My uncle was yelling at him that there was an open gate two feet from him.

When I realized they were waving me off because that bag was my dad, I decided to keep walking rather than go back to the house to help my mother. I was thirteen that summer.

My father survived with only a broken leg, two broken arms, and a broken nose. He said that as he fell, he had just enough time to think, "I'm dead, so it's all up to you, God." He relaxed, and it probably saved his life. He was still in our small neighborhood hospital about five or six blocks from our house when Hurricane Carla hit.

According to the National Weather Service, this category five hurricane was the most intense to make landfall in Texas in the twentieth century. At Port Lavaca, sustained winds of 110 miles per hour were recorded with gusts up to 153 miles per hour before the equipment was blown away. The largest evacuation in the United States was initiated because Hurricane Audrey, in 1957, had caused over 500 million dollars in property damage in Texas and Louisiana. Forty-six deaths and four hundred injuries were reported.

It hit the Texas gulf coast on September 11, 1961 and dissipated on September 17 after crossing Canada, Ontario, and Labrador. It caused flooding in basements as far north as Chicago and caused Lake Michigan to rise five feet. Carla spawned eighteen tornadoes, ten in Louisiana and eight in Texas, that caused damage as far away as Kansas.

My mother and I were alone in our home and she thought it would be a good idea for us to walk to the hospital to check on my dad because the winds might blow our big car off the road. The logic seemed a little fuzzy to me. Just being a smaller target wouldn't guarantee that we too would not be blown off the road. Besides, what else might be blowing onto that road? I had enough experience to know that I was not going to change her mind.

I have seen movies where a character confronts the lunatic holding a knife or gun and tells him or her, "You are crazy, and I'm going to call the police." The person may try to trick the other person with some lame excuse that a child could see through, such as, "You can't use that gun. You don't have a valid license." It always made me wonder who was the craziest. I don't remember what strategy I used to get out of going with her, but it was none of the above. My take away from that day is that she would have walked through fire for him, so what was a little hurricane to her.

When the winds started to die down, because the eye of the storm was over us, she started out the door in her nightgown and housecoat. Somehow, she made it to the hospital and back home the next day. We dressed properly and drove through the winds and rain the next morning. There was so much water, and there was nothing for me to do at the hospital, so I passed the time mopping the water that blew in through the front door with the absent janitor's mop and bucket.

VI
A Place of Healing

Mother was sent to Austin State Hospital as a last-ditch effort to save her from spiraling into what she would later describe as a dark tunnel. It would prove to be the best decision for her and our family. Austin State Hospital was founded in 1857 in Austin, Texas, and until 1925 it was called the State Lunatic Asylum. The main building was and is an imposing four-story stone structure built in the Classical Revival style. It has six large columns and spacious balconies on the three upper floors. There are eleven steps leading to the large portico entrance. Many additions with large windows were added to this building on all sides.

Over time, it seems another building or two was added in the current style. This facility is still in operation and is undergoing construction of a new main facility to open in 2023. I can only assume that in the past, this was a final home to many people with severe illness. Today, however, this is not a long-term facility, and the goal is to reintegrate the patient as soon as practical with some referrals to community care and for family support.

I believe her stay was only about three months, but that was longer than any previous treatment. It gave our family some breathing room and our father a little time to heal from his recent fall. After a few weeks, he went to visit her. Since his leg was still in a cast from mid-thigh to mid-calf, my brother-in-law Max drove him.

Towards Home

Max described their visit in some detail. He said that first they waited a long time as their credentials were checked. When the staff verified that they had a family member in the facility, they were let in through a locked door. They found themselves in a long narrow hall. Once again, time ticked slowly by, and he thought that they had either forgotten about them or decided to keep them.

When they were finally able to see her, he said it was remarkable. One of the first hallmarks of mental distress can be poor self-care. Even though she was not disheveled before, she wasn't careful with her dress and hair. Her make-up looked rushed and sometimes uneven or too thick. That day, he said, she looked so pretty. She was so gracious in her conversation and seemed peaceful and at ease.

When she came home a few weeks later, I also thought she was a different person. She could carry on a conversation and actually expressed an interest in me and what was going on in my life. Her focus was on the outside, not the inside. There was a presence of mind that I had not seen before.

Looking back to that time, from the perspective of a therapist, I am sure she must have had access to some other therapies besides medication. Perhaps there was time for psychological counseling and some kind of group therapy which helped her confront her personal demons.

I remember learning about Irvin Yalom's group therapy techniques in one of my psychology classes. He listed eleven factors that could only be accessed through group therapy. I won't list them all, but five of the factors seemed to be especially applicable to my mother's situation. They are as follows:

5 Recreation of the family group. He stated that inevitably, in group therapy, people would transfer their issues with family members onto another group member or maybe the group leader. This could be pointed out and discussed in a safe, supportive environment. Many times, this would lead to self-awareness and improved function for the patient (*client* is the accepted terminology now).

6 Universality, or the same boat phenomena. This concept could help people share their experiences and realize that they are not alone.

8 Interpersonal learning can serve to mirror actions that keep people isolated from others. The client can practice a better way of communicating and expressing his or her needs.

9 Group cohesiveness suggests that a group can offer a safe environment to explore thought processes and work our new strategies for troubling situations. I see it as a two-legged creature becoming a four or multilegged creature that can view a problem from greater heights and new perspectives.

10 relates to catharsis. Catharsis is a breakthrough moment that sometimes occurs with sudden insight and

release of pain or anger. An issue that had been buried or that an individual was formerly unaware of was brought into consciousness. It could be a real game changer. Yalom called it the "Aha" moment.

These were things my mother needed and had not previously received. I believe her lobotomy could probably have been avoided if she had longer term, meaningful therapies such as these first. I also think it must have been a safe place for her, where her mind could rest, and where maybe she was accepted without judgment.

I was fourteen when she came home from Austin and I think that I was most impressed with the items she brought home with her. She had made a ceramic ashtray out of a thick slab of clay. It was painted in a wine color and had pink roses and green leaves placed strategically about the surface. She had also made a teapot out of coiled clay rope. It was stained a light brown and had a lid. She began to crochet some, and even though the pieces were usually lopsided, they could be used as doilies to put under vases and pictures. I didn't know it at the time, but this was probably a precursor to my interest in occupational therapy, something I never knew existed.

She started to write and filled many, many tablets and spiral notebooks. They usually started the same exact way. The sun is out today or it is cloudy today. The birds are singing. Some reference to scripture was usually added and a prayer would end it.

I had just assumed that these writings were never about people, but I found one instance where I was wrong. I only found it a few weeks ago when I was looking through them before writing this book. She wrote, "Dear God take care of my girls and especially Joy because she has no faith in herself and is so angry." Since I did not know the timeline for any of these, I had no idea when it was written.

Things were certainly better, sexual issues had taken a back burner where my sisters and I were concerned, and her relationship with my father was much improved. It was probably about this time that it snowed at my grandfather and Aunt Thelma's house in Coolidge.

For some unknown reason, I was made to go with my parents to visit them and it started to snow. Snow, in that part of Texas, is only slightly less important than the Second Coming. It was getting late and people born and raised in the south are inept at driving in the snow, especially after dark.

Because of the heating situation in the house, I would have to sleep on a cot at the foot of the bed where my parents slept. A teenager's worst nightmare had come true and I was mortified.

My parents were all tucked up in that bed and giggling like a couple of kids at Christmas. In retrospect, I don't think my sisters ever had the pleasure of seeing our parents in such light-hearted joy. It is one of my fondest memories.

A few years went by. My dad said he would go to church with my mother, but it would be a church of his choosing, not the larger one my mother, sisters, and I had attended. He had met the pastor of a small Baptist church in town on one of his jobs and was invited to visit. We started to attend, and my dad was baptized one Sunday, which of course made my mother's world complete. Business was good, and they were planning a trip to Florida after he closed on his next big job.

VII
Earthquakes

Finding my true love was like falling through the top of a tree. You are hit by a lot of branches on the way down and suffer a lot of bumps and bruises until you land safely on a limb that can hold your weight and all the baggage that falls with you.

Dan was my first love, a fellow musician who played a trombone. On our first date when I was fifteen, we went to the movies. My girlfriends knew where we were going, and they sat behind us for the entire movie. For almost two years, we dated until he quit school and joined the Navy. I think I was really relieved. I returned his ring and he threw it at me, but came back later and picked it up. I think he had a plan B already.

One of my friends told me that when he worked at the concession stand of our local drive-in, he was seen in the back seat of a car with a classmate's older sister. He said he was so sorry and would cut off his right arm for me. I did not want his arm and he could keep it with the rest of his sorry self.

At the beginning of my junior year, I met someone I really cared for and love was feeling real. I will call him James, but that was not his real name. His sister was the girl Dan was with at the movies. James played a clarinet in the band, but he didn't march on the field with us because he had polio as a child, and his gait could be unsteady. He was not able to execute the sharp turns and about faces we made as we performed.

I started working at a donut shop on the weekends and usually got home too late to go out. James asked my parents if we could go to a late-night movie at the drive-in. Baptist kids didn't usually go to drive-in movies. Families went, but not many teenagers because of all the trouble they could get into. To my surprise, they said yes, and he picked me up after work. He had thought of everything. He packed a cooler with drinks and sandwiches, and we were set. I was sure my hair smelled of doughnuts, but we had a nice time, without the back seat wrestling that occurred around us.

James had black hair and the most beautiful sky-blue eyes. He was funny sometimes and I thought his smile would melt an iceberg. Sometimes he would stand in front of me and hold my hands in his. He was a few inches taller than me, and he would stretch out his arms causing me to pull into his chest. The only issue we had was his jealousy.

One of the boys that I went to church with put his hand in front of my face when we were going down the hall, and James called him out for it. We talked about it, and I thought the problem was solved.

After we dated a few more months, we went to an amusement park called Playland Park. It was a horrible day. It was the end of September, but unusually hot and humid for that time of year. Rain was coming in, and the atmosphere was dismal. The air hung like a wet blanket. We decided to go home, but on the way out, we stopped at a fortune-telling machine that told you your future when you put your penny in the slot and stepped on the scale.

The card that came out for me read something like this: "You will soon leave your current love for your Sailorman." We may not see him, but I know Satan exists and is wandering around seeking for someone to devour.

We argued all the way home, and James would not listen to any reasoning from me. I reassured him over and over that he was the only one I was interested in. I didn't even know where in the world Dan was stationed and couldn't care less. James called later that evening, and we argued again over that stupid card. I was so worn down. I said, "You won't listen. I give up. Let's just cool it for a few days." He had a previous breakup with a girl he dated before he met me. Maybe there was residual pain from that relationship. I will never know.

Later that night, my father came into my room and said I should get dressed. We would need to go down to the police station. James had shot himself. I spent that night at my sister Trisha's house. James's mother called, and I told her the story. Of course, it didn't help. His older sister was the only one at his funeral to acknowledge me. I remember that she put her arms around me, and we cried together.

Mother said that she used to talk to James when he called for me and I was not home. He had told her how some of the other boys at school made fun of him because of his walk. His polio had left him with an odd sway in his hips. They suggested it was effeminate and not in a kind way. I never knew about these conversations or about the guys who teased him until after his death. Mother said she tried to reassure him that he was indeed a handsome young man and maybe the other boys were a little jealous. Her sufferings had given her a sense for the sufferings of others, and even a lobotomy had not dulled her sense of humanity. I would see this come into play again and again over the coming years.

My mother was concerned that I would be blamed for his death by the kids at school. I wasn't worried. I was a zombie. I lost weight and wandered through the next few months in a daze. Only once did I break down, when one of the girls put her hand on my shoulder in the instrument room of the band hall. I know I became snarky and bitter.

I was critical of everyone. One of the boys I sat next to in class and had gone to school with forever called me out for criticizing our band president. I guess my bitterness showed more than I realized. Maybe that was why I got that honorable mention in my mother's notebook. I was angry and had no confidence in myself.

I was jolted out of this self-absorption by the next big event in our lives. I think I always harbored the fear somewhere in my soul that I would be left to care for my mother on my own. Little did I know that the treasures she poured into my life would more than compensate for any burden I may have felt.

James died in October and in March, my father was sent to the hospital with gallbladder problems. He was in that same neighborhood hospital that my mother had walked to during Hurricane Carla. We, my mother and I, were there. I had to go to school the next day and I was going to put curlers in my hair in one of the bathrooms. My dad asked me to stay, and I said I would be right back. As I stood there looking in the mirror, a sense came over me that I needed to go back into that room and sit with my father. I did.

A few days later, Cindy showed up at the high school and checked me out. Our father had passed away from an aortic aneurysm. I know this will seem odd, but somehow, I felt a strange release. That which I feared most had come upon me, and I was still standing.

Mother wanted me to sleep in their bed with her the first night after his death, but I just couldn't. I made a pallet on the floor and slept there next to her.

Life rolled on, and she was not the burden on my life that I had anticipated. I went to school at the University of Houston for two days a week as a psychology major (imagine that). I worked downtown at a title company for the other three days. Social Security gave me eighty dollars a month. I bought a Nash Rambler that had push buttons for shifting gears. On payday Fridays, I bought Cokes and Fritos for us, and we had onion dip too.

Backtracking a few months to the very last week of my senior year in high school, I was introduced to David by our mutual friend Gloria. I remembered him from our sophomore year when I had a biology class with him, but I did not think he remembered me. Our teacher Mr. V. said David and a girl named Deloris had killed our frog by overfeeding him with too many flies. He denied this vehemently. We were going to dissect the poor thing anyway, and it would sit in formaldehyde until it was needed.

David was the most uncomplicated person I ever met. I don't mean he was simple minded, just black and white stubborn. He was tall, blond, and weighed about two hundred pounds. He played football, but was more of a nerd than a jock.

After we dated for a few months, my friend Amy called

and asked me if she could ask David to take her to apply for a job in Houston. He was the only one of us who had a car then and I thought. *Well, I don't own him.* I said, "Sure. It's up to him, not me."

About thirty minutes later, there was a knock on the door. I was wearing cut-off blue jeans and a sleeveless shirt. Curlers were in my hair and I was babysitting my three-year-old nephew Brad. David was at the other end of that knock and he seemed a little irate. Ushering us out the door, he insisted that we go with him. He wanted to know, more or less, why I was so free about sharing him with my girlfriend. I tried to tell him that I trusted him and she or he didn't need my permission for anything.

When the three of us arrived at Amy's house, I was surprised to see this cute little blond dressed in a lacy, pink suit that fit her perfectly. She was wearing almost stiletto heels and her hair was perfectly arranged. I thought, *Gee Amy, aren't you a little overdressed for a work interview?* It began to dawn on me that she may have been looking for more than a ride to work. David must have known this from the get-go. The three of us—David, Brad, and I—must have made an odd picture sitting in the waiting room while Amy was interviewed. She got the job, of course, and I think my heart had sealed the deal for me that day.

David assumed a lot. He told me after our second or third date, "If we should fall in love and want to get married, I have to finish two years of college first." I told him in no uncertain terms that I was getting a four-year degree and he was getting way ahead of himself. We were married the next year.

The Vietnam War was on and David was trying to find a job in computers, but no one would hire him because he could be drafted at any time. His uncle, who had been in the CIA, told him that he should enlist rather than wait to be drafted. That way, he could choose his training and could get a stateside assignment. He chose missile tracking radar and didn't have to do a tour in 'Nam.

He headed for boot camp in Louisiana and I ordered our wedding invitations. His training time was extended and I had them reprinted once free of charge. When his training was extended for the second time, I would have to pay for the reprint. With no extra money, I just crossed out the date, wrote in the new one, and mailed them.

We had picked out our rings and planned to get them two weeks before the wedding. Since he was stuck at Fort Polk and couldn't get home, he sent me the money for the rings with his first paycheck. I took the eighty dollars, exchanged our rings for cheaper ones, and gave him back forty dollars. What a girl, if I do say so myself. Turns out, we would need that forty -dollars. This was all a harbinger of things to come.

This was the sixties, and there were racial tensions as

well as the war. Sometimes, a young man who had a run-in with the law could enlist rather than spend time in jail. One young man had done this. When he learned that some of the white guys were getting stateside duty and he was probably going to 'Nam, he blew up the night before graduation and two days before our wedding. He said he would rather go to Leavenworth than Vietnam.

He and two of his buddies pulled David's bunk mate off the top bunk and filled his mouth with shaving cream. They proceeded to hit him in the stomach to make him breathe it in. David got up and tried to get the shaving cream out of his mouth, and the fight was on. He had two black eyes and a broken jaw tooth for our wedding. People joked about what I had to do to get him there. They had a court martial that morning, and David had to attend. His parents drove him home from Louisiana, barely making it before my Uncle Billy Jack, Aunt Bobbie's husband, ran me down the aisle.

David had asked his cousins not to decorate our car but, of course, they had ignored him. When we pulled into our hotel and got out of the car, a drunk lady staggered by on the arm of a man who was only a little steadier. She said, "Oh look at the cute little soldier boy" in a loud voice. He wouldn't hit a woman, but I probably should have decked her. Needless to say, our first night together was challenging.

We left in two weeks for his first duty station in California. I had read somewhere in a magazine that if you wrapped a roast in several layers of aluminum foil and put it on the manifold of your car, you would have dinner cooked when you reached your destination. Well, we didn't have a roast, but we had a can of spaghetti and meatballs. I placed it carefully on the manifold, propping it up with tin foil to keep it from rolling around. The first town we stopped at didn't have a motel so we drove on. Just a few more miles and we would stop. The first motel we came to had a "no vacancy" sign, so we drove on. When we finally stopped for the night, the spaghetti was scorched and stuck to the inside of the can. We ate it anyway. The place was a fleabag, but it was all we could find. Whether the linens were clean or not seemed iffy. Even the roaches refused the blacked tomato sauce we left in the can. We were both so sick.

A day or so later, we stopped at a place somewhere between Texas and California, in Colorado. It was early in the afternoon and cool for late August. We were high in the mountains and had stopped early because the brakes on the car were overheating. There was a dense fog and we almost missed a roadblock where the road had been washed out. Out of nowhere, a neon sign appeared that read "Cabins for Rent." We turned off the road and found a sprinkling of small cabins nestled among the pines. The one we rented was very small. There was just enough room for a bed, a desk, a chair, and a small bath with a shower. It was neat and clean though, and there was a small store with a grill just a few miles down the country road.

Since it was still early, no other cars were there and it felt like we were the only two people in the world. We were nineteen. All the stress of the last year was behind us. The rest of our lives was before us. The remainder of that day and most of the next was spent in that little one-room cabin learning about each other, wrapped in each other arms and learning how to love. God had given us a great gift and nothing or no one could ever separate us. We drifted off to sleep on the wings of angels.

VIII
Haight-Ashbury or Finding Our Place in the World

I was driving the car, and David was sleeping in the passenger seat when we pulled onto the curb in Fairfield, California, his first duty station. I mean this literally. A tire blew out, but since I was only going about thirty miles an hour, I was able to steer into a vacant spot on the sidewalk. David opened the door and stepped out, thinking it was reveille. If it had happened when we were on the open road, it could have been a real catastrophe.

We settled in and on his first day off, we decided to go see San Francisco. We knew the song, but didn't wear any flowers in our hair. Since we were two greenhorns from Texas and knew nothing about the layout of the city, we just sort of meandered with the other cars and looked at the architecture. We found ourselves at the corner of Haight and Ashbury Streets. Although we were unaware of its significance at the time, this district was the home of the current counterculture revolution in our nation. It was where "Hell no, we won't go" began. We couldn't figure out how to navigate the traffic so we wound up circling the block with the other cars twice. If we had circled the block one more time with windows open, we would have been high into the next week.

There were many young people our age and a few years older sitting on the sidewalk, leaning against the buildings, smoking. It was late August and many guys had on shorts without shirts or shoes. This may have been the birthplace of "No shirt, no shoes, and no service." You could spin that in a lot of ways. The girls didn't have much more on, except for one. She was a tall, thin, red-headed girl with thick hair half way down her back. She was wearing a long, flowing Elizabethan dress. It was purple with long sleeves and many petticoats underneath. She wandered about in a daze and seemed totally unaware of the heat.

Janis Joplin and The Grateful Dead would begin their journey into fame from here. It was 1967 and the beginning of the young, thoughtful generation that grew out of idle college kids who would question everything in our country, except their own LSD-guided tour into oblivion. I am sure many of them are members of the Congress today.

This is where our nation started to unravel. Woodstock would follow in August of 1969. I understand the right to question our country's entrance into war and how many might oppose it out of what they considered to be unnecessary intervention into another country's politics. However, like our Democratic party today, there was no room for the opinion of others. When the veterans of Vietnam came home, these elite, new agers would spit in their faces. They were shunned, and there was no regard for those who came home injured or those who had given their lives to the service of others.

Pay was probably lower than moral. It had been said that the Army takes care of its own. All the new E1 recruits got a frozen turkey and trimmings for Christmas that year (1967) and I, in my naiveté, was ashamed, because it felt like charity.

I made a centerpiece for our coffee table out of a milk carton, which I cut into the shape of a sleigh and painted red. I made eight reindeer out of pipe cleaners and aluminum foil, tied them to the sleigh with white ribbon, and put candy in it. The only thing it lacked was Santa on the seat. Our neighbor's family was coming up to visit, and she asked if she could use it for her table centerpiece. I was so pleased that someone else thought it was cute, and I gave it to her.

We were stationed in California, Alaska, Arizona, and Fort Hood, Texas. We were world travelers by the time we moved back home seven years later. There were four notable events that I think are worth repeating.

One had to do with David's job as a missile-tracking radar specialist. There was a blip on his screen one afternoon. He saw it and reported it to his supervisors. It was determined to be of Russian origin, and our alert system moved up a few notches on the DEFCON scale before the missile retreated out of our air space. World War III was literally on our doorstep, and David had saved the world. We joked about it later, but who knows what simply doing our jobs can mean. We always see the results of our mistakes, but seldom see the good that comes from doing things right.

The second important event was the birth of our daughter. We named her Bonny Jeane. I liked a song from the movie *The Prime of Miss Jean Brodie*, made from a book by the author Muriel Spark. One verse went, "Run if you will, to the top of the hill and run into my arms Bonny Jeane." She was born in Alaska. Coming in almost two weeks overdue and weighing over nine pounds, she had hair over her ears that was almost black.

I just knew someone had switched my baby with an Athabascan. They were the indigenous tribe of Cook Inlet. All the other babies in my family had been a little scrawny. I wondered if some young native woman was looking into the face of her baby and pondering how that skinny little fair-skinned child could be hers.

The mystery was solved when the nurse said that, except for her hair, she looked so much like David he could have had her without me. Could have saved me some trouble! By the time she was two, she was a cute little blond with hair down to her shoulders and I was glad we kept her.

In Arizona, I became pregnant again and when we all got the flu, I miscarried. Afterwards, a D&C (dilation and curettage) was done, but all the "pieces" were not cleared. A few weeks later, I started to hemorrhage and was sent back to the hospital. David's major took Bonny home to his wife. I think she may have enjoyed her a little. They had all boys in their family and when their fifth son was born, the major told his wife, "Well, honey, it's another one with outdoor plumbing."

Event number three was a result of that miscarriage. I had almost waited too long and was in need of an immediate transfusion. As I lay there on the gurney, I was enveloped in a brilliant light, but it didn't hurt my eyes. I was not worried about David or Bonny, and there was an almost euphoric feeling of peace. I had the strange sensation that I was somewhere above the room. I could see the doctor, the gurney, and myself. I had been given no drugs and the transfusion had not started yet. This all dissipated as treatment began.

People have told me that this happened because I was losing consciousness, but I have filed it away in my mind as what I believe Heaven will be like: no worry, no pain, and being enveloped in the loving brightness of an all-encompassing God.

The last event was probably the catalyst for what would become David's occupation for the next twenty-eight years. One night just before bedtime, a car drove past our quarters at a high rate of speed. You don't speed on a military base. A woman was leaning out of a back window screaming. David ran out the door, climbed in our car, and chased the car down. The woman was laughing when he stopped them, and it was all a dumb stunt. When he got home, he put on his pajamas and blue terry robe. As he walked into our bedroom, I noticed he had a toy silver badge pinned to his chest. He held his rifle across his stomach and there was a Barney Fife crazed grin on his face.

When he finished his enlistment, we moved home to Texas and David joined the Houston Police Department. Of course, he had many stories to tell, but this one had to do with Good Pasture, a grain elevator near where we lived. Sometimes the grain particles in a storage facility become airborne like dust, and any small spark, such as a short in a switch or even lightning, can cause an explosion.

We lived in Galena Park and David was on his way to work when Good Pasture blew up. He would have to pass it on his way so he drove to the site to see if he could help. The fire department had pulled up, and they were looking frantically for an open entrance without much luck. David took out his gun and shot the lock off a nearby gate.

Sheet metal sections were blown about the site, and there

weren't enough stretchers for the injured people. David found a sheet that was barely attached to another with a few loose rivets. He popped those remaining rivets, and then he and the EMS crew began to use it to carry the casualties to the arriving ambulances. It was devastating to many families.

David received an Officer of the Year award, and when the presenter was reading the report, he came to a section where it was written that David had ripped two pieces of sheet metal apart to use as a stretcher. He stopped reading and looked at him out of the corner of his eye. David just shrugged his shoulders and the whole room burst into laughter.

He was twenty-seven and had only been on the job a few months. Later, one of his sergeants would tell him that there were a lot of older, more experienced men on the force who had never received such an honor, and he should not do it again.

After our two boys were born and the youngest was in the second grade, I began to feel depressed. I was a little jealous of David's job. Most people still respected the police back then, and he had a good reputation. He didn't drink, smoke, or chase women. He didn't even swear, however, our oldest son, William, used to say, "Daddy's in a good mood, he must have gotten to hit somebody today." I know this sounds heartless, but most people have no concept of what it is like to deal with children in adult bodies on the one hand and sheer evil on the other.

I worked part time at a junior college and was looking through a catalog of careers when I came across a definition of occupational therapy. These therapists grew out of the "basket weavers" that helped the wounded and "shell shocked" soldiers returning from World War I.

They used purposeful activity to help people heal. Instead of telling a person to lift weights while the person sat in a chair, they would have the person paint a picture (maybe with a weight on his or her arm). The person might sand and paint a piece of furniture or work with leather, using a tooling stamp and a hammer.

I thought about the ceramic pieces Mother had brought home with her from Austin and those repetitive stories she wrote. Her lopsided doilies and volunteer work gave her life purpose.

If we are made in God's image and one of the first things he told us about was His act of creation, then we must be creative beings too. Satan's modus operandi is destruction.

I think the COVID lockdowns did a lot to further our nation's decline creatively and morally, but I believe that we have been on the path of spiritual decline since my generation took the reins in the sixties and early seventies.

With the internet as our only companion, many of us were lulled into a dull nirvana with video games. We turned off our ability to think for ourselves, being spoon-fed our daily ration of fear and anxiety. We lost touch with other people and became incredibly selfish and childlike. We gave our independence up along with our responsibility.

In contrast, our parents (the greatest generation), were probably so great because they found themselves in such perilous, uncertain times. There was no government to "throw them a bone," since we needed every dime for the war effort. They kept their independence by shouldering their responsibilities.

They prayed, and I believe God heard them, blessing our nation beyond all expectations. However, like the lepers in the Bible, few, maybe one in ten, returned to say, "Thank you."

I don't understand how their children—my

generation—became so divided, but we were and are. I believe the dividing line is a line of faith. Some of us still believe that God is our creator, and others believe that they are their own creators. This current generation has taken it a step further.

Many young women think that they are responsible for that first cell division, not God, so they have the right to destroy it. My generation offered the pill, IUDs (intrauterine devices), and various forms of contraception to give women the freedom that they thought was, unfairly, reserved for men. In truth, they gave men release from their responsibilities to care for their families and women took on the whole yoke that was meant to be shared.

In God's condemnation of Israel (Jeremiah 2:34), Jeremiah wrote, "Also, in their skirts is found the blood of the poor innocents. I have not found it by secret search." He did not have to look hard back then and today many young women are loud and proud about their "right" to abort their children. If Abel's blood cried out to God after he was murdered by his brother Cain, how deafening the sound must be of the blood of the millions of children killed in this way.

As our young women kill within their bodies, our young men kill outside the body in those lawless cities that our government has created. Satan is polishing that same old apple, telling people that they can have all the intelligence and power in the world if they will just bite. He knows his time is short, so he is changing up his rhetoric.

In the preface to his book *The Screwtape Letters*, C.S. Lewis wrote, "There are two equal and opposite errors into which our race can fall about devils. One is to disbelieve in their existence. The other is to believe and to feel an excessive interest in them. Readers are advised to remember that the devil is a liar."[1]

I believe that most of the current generation is miserable. They can't escape the dysphoria they feel. *Maybe I was born in the wrong body. This one feels so uncomfortable. Maybe I was meant to be a man or a woman and nature made a mistake. I know I could be happier if only...*

One of the drumbeats that resound in my head is my mother's often repeated phrase, "Learn to be content." This is a whole lot harder than it sounds. It is a restating of God's message in the book of Matthew. We can't add an inch to our height by thinking about it and we can't change tomorrow by worrying about it. He says that even the hairs of our head are numbered. Now, if God thinks we are important enough to number our hairs, then what are we worried about?

I have lived long enough to know that how I present myself, what I own, or who I hold in my arms will not bring me happiness. Things wear out. We wear out. We lose our

---

[1] C.S. Lewis, *The Screwtape Letters* (New York: Harper One, 1996), page.

homes in floods, fires, and market turn-downs. People die, or just leave.

There is, however, a balm in Gilead, as the song goes, but we can only share it if the other person is willing to take it into his or her own hand. We are not passive, but active in receiving His gift.

God is there, ready to forgive and comfort us in our distress. He will not, however, give His kingdom over to those with reprobate minds. If God accepted us without a change to our sinful natures, heaven would be taken over by evil.

In Revelations 12, John tells us that there is war in heaven today between Michael and the angels of God and Satan and his angels. He states that Satan will fail and be cast down into a pit. He will no longer be able to accuse us to God or deceive the world. The blood of Christ is the poison that finally defeats the enemy of humankind. In Ephesians, we read, "For we wrestle not against flesh and blood, but against principalities, against powers, against the rulers of the darkness of this world, against spiritual wickedness in high places" (6:12 KJV).

IX
Finishing the Race

For almost twenty years after my father died, my mother lived alone. My sisters and I looked after her, but she paid her own bills, bought her own groceries, and attended church. She taught teenaged girls in Sunday school for a few years. Several small three-by-five inch school photos were arranged on those lopsided crotched doilies on an end table in her living room. A few of them had written sweet sentiments on the back expressing how much they had learned in her class and they were signed with love.

Rebuilding her life, she joined a support group called The Shoulder. I remember visiting one afternoon as she was getting ready for her meeting. She put on some of her best clothes and high-heeled shoes and arranged her hair. A man about her age picked her up and she smiled graciously as she slid into the front seat of his car. She sold burial insurance policies over the phone and received an award as top saleswoman a few months. There was local TV game show called Dialing for Dollars and she went there with a group of ladies from a woman's charity organization. She was chosen out of the audience and made it on stage, but didn't win. She also volunteered at a hospital for a year or so. They sent her home from this job, but I am most proud of her for the event that let up to her dismissal.

My sister had kept the five-year-old daughter of one of her friends for a short time. This little girl had cerebral palsy and I remember the white lace socks and black patent leather shoes that she wore over her leg braces. Cerebral palsy can cause tight ligaments and the legs may scissor. This can cause irritation, especially in the thigh area. When this little girl became a teenager, she was admitted to the hospital where my mother volunteered. Scissoring had caused severe irritation to her upper thigh area and she required treatment to heal the wound.

Since my mother knew the girl, she would talk with her and help her with her food tray or whatever else she might need as she made her rounds on the unit. Some sort of adaptive equipment was constructed for her. The aim was to keep her legs separated as she healed. On one occasion, when my mother entered her room, she was exposed and there was no way for the young girl to cover herself. My mother went to the busy nurses' desk and demanded that they see to her immediately. She would not leave until it was done. She caused such a stir about the loss of dignity for this young lady that they sent her home. She got her point across and maybe the incident made a much-needed impression on the staff.

In order to finish my mother's story, I have to go back to mine because they intertwine, as all generational stories do. I was hesitant to apply for occupational therapy school because it was a five-year degree. Even though I had some pre-requisites, I would be forty years old before I finished. Someone told me I would be forty years old anyway, so with the encouragement of David and the kids, I went back to school.

Most of my career was spent in early intervention, in the public schools and teaching at junior colleges, but my first three years were spent on the geriatric psych ward at Harris County Psychiatric Center in Houston. It was amazing to me how different and "normal" the patients (the word *client* is the correct terminology now) seemed when we took them outside to smoke or get some fresh air.

We talked about children, ideas, and sometimes cooking. On the unit, they would assume the role. Many, although not all, would become withdrawn and passive in that setting. They called it becoming institutionalized. One lady, however, who cleaned her chicken with bleach, did seem to be true to herself wherever she was.

Mother had wanted to talk with the people on the unit to encourage them. After I was there for about two years, I received permission from my supervisor to let her visit one of our group therapy sessions. Many years on Thorazine had left her with Parkinson's-like symptoms and she needed a wheelchair.

I had not expected her reaction when I wheeled her onto the unit and the door was locked behind us. Her expression became like one of the patients. Maybe she feared she was being admitted again. It was a small group and, somehow, we made it through. She did not breathe easily until we were in the car again and on the way home.

Years ago, the psychiatrists had told us that our mother probably would never improve. They said that schizophrenia is a progressive disease with a deteriorating course. I have heard that it's a downhill slide for all of us after puberty. Much of the last fifteen years of her life was spent with my sister Trisha, with my family, or in a nursing home when she became physically feeble

When she was about sixty-five, she decided that she was well and did not need the SSI disability check that gave her a few dollars above her regular Social Security allotment. She wrote to the government and the powers that be responded that, of course, they would be glad to end her supplemental income and she would have to pay back the previous twelve years. She could not and we felt, on principal, she should not be required to do that.

A court date was set, and we all testified on her behalf.

David did such a good job of describing what it was like to be her son-in-law and deal with her idiosyncrasies that I think they wanted to reinstate her supplement and maybe give her a raise. Maybe they thought he should have the money. In the end, they did stop her SSI, but she was not required to pay any of it back.

At one point, after she lived with us a little while, she needed more physical care and wanted to go back to a nursing home she had been in previously. Two representatives from her last placement came out to interview her about coming back and turned her down.

I think I had inadvertently put schizophrenia instead of mental illness on the list of problems that you are required to fill out for admission. This made me think it was my fault that she was rejected. She did, however, have a prior run-in with a nurse's aide at that facility. The aide had accused her of wearing some else's house shoes. When she attempted to take them off her feet, there was an altercation.

When Mother stayed with my sister for a while, Trisha thought she needed to be recommitted or at least reevaluated for a change in her meds. After the pre-admission interview, they said Mother was fine and did not need any psychiatric intervention.

People can use an illness, mental or physical, to manipulate and get their way. It had become a test of wills between my sister and mother. Trisha won that time, and she moved back in with us, or maybe Mother won that time. "Born for the day of adversity" sounded a whole lot less noble.

Just before she died, Mother said that she saw our father and two young men coming down the hall several times, but they wouldn't turn around and come back to her when she called them. Trisha's twenty-year-old son had died from a fall at work and his cousin, who had a congenital heart condition, died a few years later. Trisha felt that they were the ones that Mother saw.

She said, "Mother, the next time you see them, go with them." Shortly after that, Mother fell into a coma. When the doctor said she was only a few days from death, Trisha and I alternately stayed with her. We left to get something to eat when Cindy, our sister who lived several miles away, arrived. She died shortly after Cindy got there and I truly think Mother had waited for her. She was eighty-three.

My mother always had a special quality that neither my sisters nor I inherited. My cousin, Ida Joe, said she always loved our mother and felt there was something special about her. She never fit the mold and was irritating to say the least to her immediate family. Somehow, she could connect with people, often strangers or people she barely knew. Her faith was her lifeline. We learned to care from her and if we were able to choose our mother, it would have been her.

X
What I Think I Have Learned

Sometime in the days before he died, my father said he wanted to teach his girls to learn to shoulder their responsibilities. Maybe he was concerned that we wouldn't take care of our mother or maybe there was a broader meaning.

In Ecclesiastes 7:14, it says, "In the day of prosperity be joyful, but in the day of adversity consider." Could there have ever been a worse day than the day Adam and Eve were kicked out of the garden, where we find ourselves today?

God banished Satan to crawl on his belly for his deceptions, but he is still here, at least until God decides he isn't.

Genesis 3:16 lines out our punishment for disobeying God. Unto the woman he said, "I will greatly multiply thy sorrow and thy conception; in sorrow thou shalt bring forth children; thy desire shall be to thy husband and he shall rule over thee." Two points are laid out here for Eve, and by extension, all women.

As mothers, we love our children desperately, and it tears us apart to have a rebellious child. We see how it was for God to lose his precious creations to an evil force. We pray for a knock on the door and an "I'm so sorry for what I have put you through." Our punishment teaches us about our Creator and tunes us into his frequency.

As for the part about desiring our husbands, it binds us to them. Marriage was God's plan. It offers us comfort and safety and a sense of completeness here on earth. Most wives love their husbands and the claws come out when another woman tries to take him. "And he shall rule over thee" seems to be the fly in the ointment. We want to make our own decisions, but at the same time, no woman wants a doormat for a husband. Perhaps we don't trust men to make the right decision because Adam didn't.

Adam had a long stretch alone with a loving God before He gave him the one thing that he needed in his life to help him and bring him contentment: Eve. I think that Adam took Eve for granted and he used her to test the waters as Satan laid out his deceptive plan.

Adam could have said, "Eve, don't listen to that snake," instead of standing there watching to see what would happen and then joining the party. There was, conceivably, a split second when he could have saved them both or at least himself. Like so many situations in life, the first to be deceived is not generally the last to be deceived. What we don't learn from observation, we are destined to learn from experience. Maybe Adam came to love the gift (Eve) more than the giver (God) or maybe he just shirked his responsibility. At any rate, God judged them both to be culpable and not one more than the other.

Adam's punishment was all tied up with wrestling his food from a cursed earth by the sweat of his brow. As it was for Eve, this was part of a divine lesson plan. Adam, like men in general, could not control the environment and therefore could not predict a good or bad harvest. All life, from seeds to elephants, is in God's hands. We can store up, shore up, and try to predict the next disaster, but we are always in a constant battle for survival. If you don't work, you don't eat.

I am trying to make a connection here between the responsibility my father expected his daughters to shoulder and the responsibility that our heavenly father expects us to shoulder as a result of our willful disobedience. The punishment was not arbitrary. He told us the stove was hot before we ever put our hand to it. He told us obedience was required to live in His paradise. His perfect world. We chose to go our own way. He simply closed the door behind us. Illnesses such as my mother's and all the small or large and seemingly insurmountable tragedies that occur in life can probably be traced back to some wrong doing on the part of someone. But behind it all, I believe the choice our first parents made is the same one we would have made and is the crux of all our misery.

We could never again approach God and that burden would be ours for eternity. The breath of life that God breathed into Adam would be expelled at our last breath. Our connection with His spirit had been broken except for a few, random prophets of His choosing. We no longer spoke the same spiritual language. Our messages seemed to be returned unanswered.

Because we could no longer come to Him, He came to us through the only dimension we could comprehend, flesh and blood. He came to get. Like a light in a dark world, He leads the way to an open door. It is ours to walk through or ignore.

Most of the world rejects the creation story and denies any divine reunion plan. I am pretty sure that the Jewish people are the only group in history to identify one supreme being who wants to have a relationship with us. Through their family history, our families are taught about a loving God, who, like a loving parent, requires obedience.

The reason for their great trials and sufferings are not explained to us, but serve as examples of what it is like to live in a world that hates your core values. Watching the news and feeling the current anti- Christian sentiment expressed by our government in favor of sexual perversion, I and many of my fellow Christians are sure that we will be the next group to feel the backlash and hatred that our Jewish brothers and sisters have experienced.

We are imperfect. Many of the troubles we experience are of our own making, but many are not. In the final analysis, how valuable a commodity we must be for Satan to desire us as desperately as he does.

I want to share a quotation from Victor David Hanson, a commentator who frequently appears on Fox News. He referred to an old Greek idiom that went back as far as Sophocles around 441 BC: "Whom the gods would destroy, they first make mad." Satan is the god of this world and offers anxiety and confusion to those who listen to him. In contrast, our God has not given us a spirit of fear, but of power and of a sound mind (2 Timothy 1:7 NKJV).

I feel that our nation is descending into madness. Because America was seen as a guiding light or a beacon on the hill, we are infecting other nations. Truth is subjective today and whatever the mind can conceive is accepted. We are drowning in a sea of our own excrement and think it's the Bahamas.

The "let the child find his or her own way" and "everyone gets a trophy" attitude has morphed into lawlessness and the destruction of our nation. There cannot be a "no fault" society. We must all be accountable for our own actions, and any government that decides it will not punish the crimes of individuals will not hold its leaders accountable either.

There is a spirit of evil that is deceiving our younger generation today. The black youth are told they have been cheated by the white, so they are free to steal and destroy. They are by no means alone in this aggression, but they are in the majority in the major cities. The white youth are told that they are irreparably guilty and must bear the sins of their fathers. None of it is true.

Hebrews 4:12 tells us that God's word is a sword, and it judges the thoughts and attitudes of the heart. In Luke 17:1, Jesus tells his disciples that offenses will come, but woe to him through whom they come. We are all responsible to keep our own noses clean. You don't get a pass because you have trouble. We all have trouble. Each of us knows his own misery.

What else do I think I know? Difficulties make us stronger. Warts make us more interesting. God has plans for our lives and so does Satan.

Our situations in life may be difficult on many levels, but God sprinkles us with just enough joy to clue us in to what it will be like when we get to sit at his feet. We can't fix the past or know the future. The here and now can be incredibly dull, especially if you are alone. There is strength in numbers. Life is often a waiting game.

I believe that, except for a small portion, we are currently raising a generation of weak, desperately unhappy, faithless young people. We have told them that life is easy and with the touch of a button or screen, all their wishes can be granted. We have lied to them and robbed them of the glory that comes from a fight well fought.

Life is not easy. We are "out of the garden" and no amount of paint and camouflage can fix it. If you try to analyze the Ten Commandments, you may come to the conclusion that only in caring for others do we care for ourselves. The Commandments are guideposts, not stop signs.

We may be wrong, but many people feel that our descent into chaos is increasing exponentially. Evil has always existed and societies have fallen before, but this is worldwide. Daily, people are being blinded to what is right and, in some cases, just plain logical. Our crisis is such that it can only be solved with divine intervention.

Genesis suggests that God's initial plan, before the fall and again after the flood, was for humans to spread out and inhabit the world. It appears that we have spread out, cut it up in little pieces, and fought to keep our pieces to ourselves. A world united under one government seems like a good idea, but the word *government* should be a clue to that misconception. If you can name a government on the face of the earth that is not corrupt, including ours, you are either delusional or have a stake in the game. Only when Christ returns and the government is on His shoulders will there be peace among the people. Until then, we are told to pray for our leaders. We are such a mixed bag of the power hungry and those that truly wish to serve and it is often impossible to tell the difference.

At the beginning of my story, I talked about a ring for my Aunt Clearcy hidden behind a picture. The question was which picture: the one of the family or the one of Christ?

We look back to our families for clarity. The current fad is to find our roots to help us define who we are. Christians believe if we go back far enough, we will discover that we are all one enormous extended family. I looked up the definition of a ring and it is a symbol of unity, the self, wealth, status, family, and devotion.

A ring is also the symbol of infinity, eternity, wholeness, and perfection. Scripture says we were in the mind of God before we were born and death is not the end of the soul. The question is where will we spend that eternity.

Both pictures suggest a ring or completeness, but only in Christ's love and sacrifice do we find true peace forever. Jesus has been gone for over two thousand years, but he left us with a comforter to teach us right from wrong. The choice is ours, and I will wrap myself in that comforter and listen for my name to be called, whether it is whispered in my ear alone or trumpeted for a mass exodus.

Bibliography

Lewis, C.S. *The Screwtape Letters*. New York: Harper One, 1996.

Yalom, Irvin with Leszcz, Molyn. *The Theory and Practice of Group Psychotherapy*. New York: Basic Books, A Member of the Perseus Books Group, 2005

Milton Keynes UK
Ingram Content Group UK Ltd.
UKHW040633310723
426074UK00001B/241